W9-CNK-854

My United States

Texas

JOSH GREGORY

Children's Press®
An Imprint of Scholastic Inc.

Content Consultant
James Wolfinger, PhD, Associate Dean and Professor
College of Education, DePaul University, Chicago, Illinois

Library of Congress Cataloging-in-Publication Data
Names: Gregory, Josh, author.
Title: Texas / by Josh Gregory.
Description: New York, NY : Children's Press, an imprint of Scholastic Inc., [2018] | Includes bibliographical references and index.
Identifiers: LCCN 2017001059 | ISBN 9780531252635 (library binding) | ISBN 9780531232934 (pbk.)
Subjects: LCSH: Texas—Juvenile literature.
Classification: LCC F386.3 .G74 2018 | DDC 976.4—dc23
LC record available at https://lccn.loc.gov/2017001059

Photos ©: cover: Panoramic Images/Getty Images; back cover ribbon: AliceLiddelle/Getty Images; back cover bottom: Witold Skrypczak/Getty Images; 3 bottom: Eric James/Alamy Images; 3 map: Jim McMahon; 4 left: Andriy Markov/Shutterstock; 4 right: Fanfo/Shutterstock; 5 top: Glenn Nagel/Dreamstime; 5 bottom: Dave Tonge/Getty Images; 7 top: SeanPavonePhoto/iStockphoto; 7 center top: Inge Johnsson/Alamy Images; 7 center bottom: robertharding/Alamy Images; 7 bottom: Andrew D. Brosig/Tyler Morning Telegraph/AP Images; 8-9: Mark Wetters Images/Getty Images; 11: Blaine Harrington/age fotostock /Superstock, Inc.; 12: PP3333/iStockphoto; 13: Minerva Studio/iStockphoto; 14: Wisanu Boonrawd/Shutterstock; 15 main: Alan Murphy/Minden Pictures; 15 inset: GizmoPhoto/Shutterstock; 16-17: Davel5957/iStockphoto; 19: Sean Kilpatrick/The Canadian Press/AP Images; 20: Tigatelu/iStockphoto; 22 right: ayzek/Shutterstock; 22 left: YAY Media AS/Alamy Images; 23 bottom left: Mark Smith/Science Source; 23 top right: Fanfo/Shutterstock; 23 bottom right: Misscanon/Dreamstime; 23 center: antpkr/iStockphoto; 23 top left: JoeLena/iStockphoto; 23 bottom center: Andriy Markov/Shutterstock; 24-25: Roy H. Anderson/Getty Images; 27: North Wind Picture Archives/The Image Works; 28: SeanPavonePhoto/iStockphoto; 29: De Agostini Picture Library/The Granger Collection; 30 right: Bob Daemmrich/The Image Works; 30 left: Roy H. Anderson/Getty Images; 31 right: Everett Historical/Shutterstock; 31 left: SeanPavonePhoto/iStockphoto; 31 center: YAY Media AS/Alamy Images; 32: jdwphotos/iStockphoto; 33: Everett Collection/Superstock, Inc.; 34-35: Glenn Nagel/Dreamstime; 36: Richard Ellis/Alamy Images; 37: Gabriel Perez/Getty Images; 38: Bloomberg/Getty Images; 39 background: f11photo/Thinkstock; 39 inset: Dean Fikar/Shutterstock; 40 background: PepitoPhotos/iStockphoto; 40 bottom: Fanfo/Shutterstock; 41: Mike Heffner/Getty Images; 42 top left: RDA/Tallandier/Getty Images; 42 top right: Bettmann/Getty Images; 42 center left: The Granger Collection; 42 center right: Paul Natkin/Getty Images; 42 bottom: Kathy Hutchins/Shutterstock; 43 top left: J.J Guillen/EPA/Newscom; 43 top right: Jason LaVeris/Getty Images; 43 center left: Gregorio T. Binuya/Everett Collection; 43 center right: Stefanie Keenan/Getty Images; 43 bottom left: Dave Tonge/Getty Images; 43 bottom center: Larry Busacca/PW/Getty Images; 43 bottom right: Marc Nader/ZUMA Wire/Alamy Images; 44 bottom: Inge Johnsson/Alamy Images; 45 top: Mark Wetters Images/Getty Images; 45 bottom: Mike Heffner/Getty Images; 45 center: RDA/Tallandier/Getty Images.

Maps by Map Hero, Inc.

SCHOLASTIC, CHILDREN'S PRESS, A TRUE BOOK™, and associated logos are trademarks and/or registered trademarks of Scholastic Inc., 557 Broadway, New York, NY 10012.
1 2 3 4 5 6 7 8 9 10 R 27 26 25 24 23 22 21 20 19 18

Front cover: Two riders in Hunt at sunset
Back cover: An oil well near Alice

Welcome to Texas

Find the Truth!

Everything you are about to read is true *except* for one of the sentences on this page.

Which one is **TRUE**?

T or F Texas was once an independent country.

T or F Texas is the largest state in the country.

Find the answers in this book.

Key Facts

Capital: Austin

Estimated population as of 2016: 27,862,596

Nickname: The Lone Star State

Biggest cities: Houston, San Antonio, Dallas

UNITED STATES

Texas

Contents

Texas-style chili

THE **BIG** TRUTH!

What Represents Texas?

Prickly pear cactus

Cadillac Ranch

Singer, songwriter, dancer, and actor Usher is from Dallas.

This Is Texas!

COLORADO

MISS

OKLAHOMA

NEW MEXICO

ARK

Canadian

AMARILLO

American Quarter Horse
Heritage Center & Museum

Red

African American
Museum

N
W · E
S

LUBBOCK

National Cowgirl
Museum and
Hall of Fame

Llano Estacado

FORT WORTH

DALLAS

Caddo Mounds
State Historic Site

EL PASO

Guadalupe
Mountains

Colorado

Texas Sports
Hall of Fame

Brazos

Trinity

4

Pecos

TEXAS

WACO

Cockrell
Butterfly
Center

Big Bend
National Park

The Alamo

Lady Bird Johnson
Wildflower Center

AUSTIN

Rio Grande

MEXICO

Texas State Capitol

HOUSTON

0   80
Miles

1

SAN
ANTONIO

Lyndon B. Johnson
Space Center

3

2

Fort McIntosh

Rio Grande

Nueces

Aransas National
Wildlife Refuge

LAREDO

CORPUS
CHRISTI

Padre Island
National
Seashore

Rio Grande Valley

BROWNSVILLE

GULF OF
MEXICO

1 The Alamo

Located in the heart of San Antonio, this historic mission and fort marks the site of an important battle in Texas's fight for independence. Even today, "Remember the Alamo" is a popular saying among Texans.

2 Big Bend National Park

Home to dramatic mountains and steep canyons, this national park draws tourists from around the world. Visitors can enjoy hiking and bicycling trails, or take a scenic drive through the park.

3 Johnson Space Center

Named for President Lyndon B. Johnson, a Texas native, the center is the hub for the National Aeronautics and Space Administration (NASA). Here, astronauts undergo training for important missions, and scientists conduct groundbreaking experiments.

4 Caddo Mounds

Between the 800s and 1300s, the Mississippian people settled at this site, where they lived in grass huts and built incredible mounds of Earth.

Guadalupe Peak is the highest point in Texas.

CHAPTER 1

Land and Wildlife

Texas is a land filled with beautiful landscapes. Although best known for its sprawling rangelands, Texas is also home to beaches, forests, swamps, and huge modern cities.

Texas ranks second in the nation in both size (after Alaska) and population (after California). But as any Texan will tell you, it's the number-one place in the world to live!

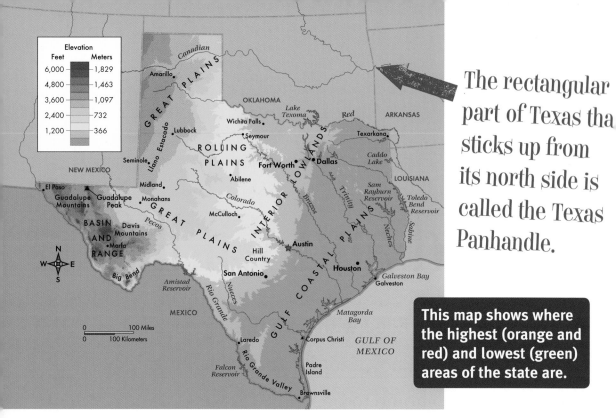

The rectangular part of Texas that sticks up from its north side is called the Texas Panhandle.

This map shows where the highest (orange and red) and lowest (green) areas of the state are.

Texas Geography

The Gulf of Mexico borders Texas on the southeast, while Mexico itself lies to the southwest. Texas also shares borders with the states of New Mexico, Oklahoma, Arkansas, and Louisiana. Much of the population is concentrated in the state's eastern half. In west Texas, you're more likely to find small towns scattered across wide-open spaces.

Big River

The southwestern border of Texas is formed by the Rio Grande. If you cross this river, you'll find yourself in Mexico. The name Rio Grande is Spanish for "big river." This is the perfect description for a river that flows 1,240 miles (1,996 kilometers) from Colorado to the Gulf of Mexico.

Hot and Cold

When people think of Texas, they often imagine a place where the weather is hot and dry. While this can be true, cold weather and precipitation are quite common in some parts of the state. For example, low temperatures and snowstorms are a normal part of winter in the panhandle and in mountainous areas. Rain is most plentiful in the eastern portion of the state. The climate generally becomes drier as you move westward.

Snow blankets the trees in Humble, a city near Houston.

MAXIMUM TEMPERATURE
120°F

MINIMUM TEMPERATURE
-23°F

Tornadoes can cause massive damage with their powerful winds.

Weather Worries

The drier parts of Texas can experience **drought** that lasts for years at a time. This causes the ground to dry out and get hard. When rain finally comes, the water pools on top instead of soaking in. This can lead to serious flooding. Texans also have to watch out for huge storms. Hurricanes are common along the Gulf Coast, and about 126 tornadoes per year strike the plains of northern Texas.

Texas Plants

An incredible range of plants grows in Texas's diverse landscapes. The state is home to more than 5,000 wildflower **species**. Wild grasses are also common. In desert areas, you can spot more than 100 different types of cactus. In forests, you'll mostly see pine trees. But you'll also find oak, ash, hickory, and many other types of trees.

Wild bluebonnet flowers grow among other wildflowers in a Texas field.

A whooping crane snatches a blue crab from the water for its meal.

Texas is home to nearly 4 million white-tailed deer.

Amazing Animals

Texas is home to many kinds of animals. More than 100 snake species live in the state, and about 200,000 alligators inhabit Texas swamps. In deserts and mountains, you might spot mountain lions and lizards. Along the coast, you'll see spoonbills, whooping cranes, and other aquatic birds. You might also notice sea turtles crawling ashore to lay their eggs. In many wild areas, you should watch out for wolves, coyotes, and bears.

The Texas capitol building is the largest in the country.

CHAPTER 2

Government

Unlike other U.S. states, Texas was once an independent country. During this time, the city of Austin was established as the capital of the **Republic** of Texas. When Texas became a part of the United States in 1845, Austin remained the state capital. Today, it is where members of the state government gather to make, enforce, and carry out Texas's laws.

TEXAS'S STATE GOVERNMENT

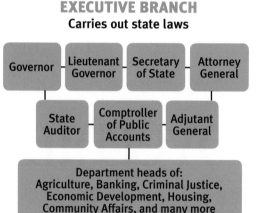

LEGISLATIVE BRANCH
Writes and passes state laws

Senate (31 members)	House of Representatives (150 members)

EXECUTIVE BRANCH
Carries out state laws

Governor	Lieutenant Governor	Secretary of State	Attorney General

State Auditor	Comptroller of Public Accounts	Adjutant General

Department heads of:
Agriculture, Banking, Criminal Justice, Economic Development, Housing, Community Affairs, and many more

JUDICIAL BRANCH
Enforces state laws

Appellate Courts (2 Divisions)

Supreme Court	Court of Appeals (14 divisio...

Trial Courts

District Courts (443 divisions)

Statutory Courts

Constitutional County Courts (254 divisions)

Justice of the Peace Courts

Municipal Courts

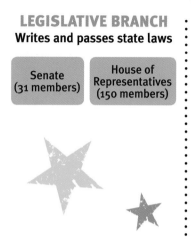

The Three Branches of Government

Texas's executive branch is headed by the governor and includes the lieutenant governor, secretary of state, and attorney general. The legislative branch is responsible for making and passing new laws for the state. It is divided into a 31-member Senate and a 150-member House of Representatives. The judicial branch enforces Texas laws by hearing court cases.

Mayor Sylvester Turner (right) presents Canadian prime minister Justin Trudeau with Houston's Key to the City.

Texas has 254 counties. That is more than any other state.

Local Leaders

Texas's towns, cities, and **counties** also have their own elected leaders. These local officials can have a big effect on day-to-day life for the people of Texas. They are responsible for local roads and transportation systems, schools, and many other important services on which people rely.

Texas in the National Government

Each state elects officials to represent it in the U.S. Congress. Like every state, Texas has two senators. The U.S. House of Representatives relies on a state's population to determine its numbers. With its large population, Texas has 36 representatives in the House.

Every four years, states vote on the next U.S. president. Each state is granted a number of electoral votes based on its number of members in Congress. With two senators and 36 representatives, Texas has 38 electoral votes.

2 senators and 36 representatives

38 electoral votes

Texas's has the second mo electoral votes of any stat Only California has more.

Representing Texas

Elected officials in Texas represent a population with a range of interests, lifestyles, and backgrounds.

Ethnicity (2015 estimates)

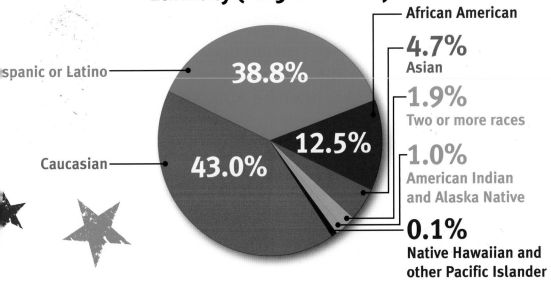

- spanic or Latino — 38.8%
- Caucasian — 43.0%
- 12.5%
- African American — 4.7%
- Asian — 1.9%
- Two or more races — 1.0%
- American Indian and Alaska Native
- 0.1% Native Hawaiian and other Pacific Islander

28% of the population have a degree beyond high school.

17% of Texas residents were born in other countries.

62% own their own homes.

85% live in cities.

82% of the population graduated from high school.

35% speak a language other than English at home.

THE BIG TRUTH!

What Represents Texas?

States choose specific animals, plants, and objects to represent the values and characteristics of the land and its people. Find out why these symbols were chosen to represent Texas or discover surprising curiosities about them.

Seal

The state seal was designed when Texas was a republic. It shows a star surrounded by olive and oak branches.

Flag

The state flag of Texas was adopted in 1839 as the national flag of the Republic of Texas. The red section stands for bravery, the white stands for purity, and the blue stands for loyalty. The single star gives the state its nickname: the Lone Star State.

Jalapeño

STATE PEPPER

Delicious as a topping on Texas-style chili or as a part of many other dishes, this spicy pepper is a classic Texas treat.

Chili

STATE DISH

This spicy meat stew is a big part of Texas's local culinary tradition.

Guitar

STATE MUSICAL INSTRUMENT

With the popularity of country and folk music in Texas, it is no surprise that the acoustic guitar is an official symbol of the state.

Monarch Butterfly

STATE INSECT

In fall, huge numbers of these beautiful insects fly through Texas on their way to spend winter in Mexico.

Texas Toad

STATE AMPHIBIAN

This toad species thrives in Texas's dry environments.

Prickly Pear Cactus

STATE PLANT

This cactus grows in Texas's many desert areas. Some varieties are even edible!

Pre-historic hunters attempt to take down a mammoth.

CHAPTER 3

History

Humans first came to the land that is now Texas sometime around 9000 BCE. These **nomadic** people used handmade spears to hunt large animals such as **mammoths** and buffalo. They also gathered food from wild plants. When they needed a place to stay, they sought out caves and other natural shelter.

The First Settlers

Eventually, the people who occupied Texas settled down to form more permanent communities. By about 700 BCE, they began planting crops. Villages and other settlements formed around these farms. People invented new tools and found other ways to improve their daily lives. Over hundreds of years, Texas's many settlements developed into a variety of unique cultures. They each had different languages and traditions.

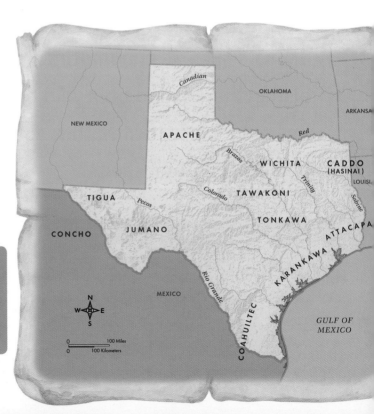

This map shows the general areas where Native American groups settled before European exploration.

Native Americans grew crops such as corn and squash.

A Land of Many Cultures

Native peoples such as the Coahuiltecs, Karankawas, and Attacapas lived along the Gulf Coast. The Caddo people of east Texas built tall, cone-shaped houses from wood and long grass. The Jumanos built houses from adobe bricks. Apaches hunted buffalo across the plains. In the 1700s, other native groups such as the Comanches would move from nearby areas and begin settling in Texas.

Changing Times

In the 1500s, Spanish explorers began traveling to America in search of wealth and land. They first reached Texas in 1528. Over the following centuries, they continued exploring and expanding their control over the region by founding **colonies** and **missions**. The Spanish worked to convert native people to their religion and way of life. Some accepted, and many others resisted. However, they could not stop Spain from taking over Texas, Mexico, and other nearby areas.

The Alamo was originally part of a Spanish mission called San Antonio de Valero. Later, in the 1800s, it was used as a fort.

Before Mexico fought for independence from Spain, Native Americans were fighting against missions set up by the Spanish government in places such as San Sabá.

Mexican Independence

By the 1800s, many people living in Spain's American colonies wanted to form their own governments. In 1821, Mexico fought and won a war for independence from Spain. Texas was included as a part of the newly formed country. To spur Mexico's growth, the new government encouraged wealthy people to move there. Settlers began flooding into Texas from the United States. Soon, they outnumbered Texas's Hispanic population.

The Texas Revolution

The people of Texas, especially the new settlers, soon became dissatisfied with the Mexican government. In 1835, they began a war to separate from Mexico and form their own independent country. Led by Texans such as Sam Houston, Stephen Austin, and Davy Crockett, they won the war in 1836 and founded the Republic of Texas. However, even after the war, Texas and Mexico continued to dispute the exact location of the border between them.

Timeline of Texas Events

1528 CE
Europeans arrive in Texas for the first time.

1821
Mexico, including Texas, wins independence from Spain.

ca. 9000 BCE → 1528 CE → 1682 → 1821

ca. 9000 BCE
Humans first arrive in the land that would become Texas.

1682
The first Texas mission is founded.

The 28th State

After gaining independence, many Texans wanted their homeland to become part of the United States. They eventually got their wish. In March 1845, Texas was officially **annexed** by the United States. It was admitted as the 28th state just a few months later, on December 29. This quickly led to a war between the United States and Mexico over the border with Texas. The United States won the war in 1848, and Mexico agreed to give up its claim to land north of the Rio Grande.

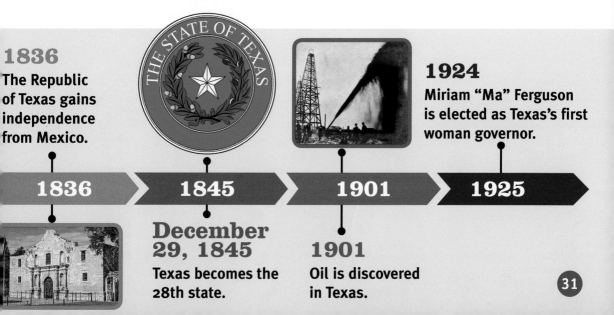

1836
The Republic of Texas gains independence from Mexico.

1924
Miriam "Ma" Ferguson is elected as Texas's first woman governor.

1836 **1845** **1901** **1925**

December 29, 1845
Texas becomes the 28th state.

1901
Oil is discovered in Texas.

Growing and Changing

In the decades following the Civil War (1861–1865), Texas grew to play a major role in the U.S. economy. Agriculture, especially cattle ranching, became a huge industry and brought many people to Texas. In 1901, oil was discovered in the state, sparking even more economic growth and drawing more new residents. Today, of all the states, Texas is second only to California in both population and the size of its economy.

Nearly 99 percent of farms and ranches in Texas are owned by families, small partnerships, or family-run companies.

Sam Houston

During the Texas Revolution, Sam Houston led the Texan army into battle against Mexico. Afterward, he was chosen to be the first president of the Republic of Texas. As president, Houston supported Texas joining the United States. After statehood, he became a U.S. senator and later served as the governor of Texas. However, he was thrown out of office at the start of the Civil War because he did not want Texas to join the **Confederacy**. He died just a few years later, before the war was over.

Cadillac Ranch is a piece of art in Amarillo. Visitors are encouraged to bring spray cans and leave their mark on the colorful, constantly-changing cars.

CHAPTER 4

Culture

Texas is a unique place with a culture that sets it apart from any other U.S. state. This comes largely as a result of its great diversity. People from many different backgrounds live in Texas. Elements of Mexican and Native American cultures mix with traditions brought by other people who have settled in Texas over the years. Cowboy themes, Mexican American traditions, and Native American culture are all popular topics among Texas writers and artists.

Crazy About Sports

Texans enjoy watching and playing many sports. However, they love football more than any other. Texans follow pro teams such as the Houston Texans and the Dallas Cowboys. They also enjoy watching the state's many college and high school teams. In addition to football, many Texans appreciate a good rodeo. In this traditional sport, cowboys test their skills in a variety of events, including bull riding and calf roping.

Rodeos can be dangerous, but they are also a lot of fun to watch.

Texas Celebrations

Texans celebrate many local holidays and events. Each year from October 31 until November 2, many Texans participate in Día de los Muertos (Day of the Dead) festivities. Rooted in Mexican traditions, this holiday is based

Colorful skull decorations and costumes are a big part of Día de los Muertos celebrations.

on remembering people who have died. Another popular annual event is the Texas State Fair. Held in September and October in Dallas, the fair celebrates Texas agriculture and local traditions.

A worker prepares to install the hood of a car at a General Motors plant in Arlington.

From the Office to the Oil Field

The agriculture and oil industries remain two of the biggest employers in Texas. Manufacturing also provides many of the state's jobs. Texans build automobiles, assemble electronics, and make chemical products. Major cities such as Houston, Austin, and Dallas offer an especially wide range of careers. There, many people work in technology, finance, scientific research, and more.

Making a Connection

Though most people in Texas live in cities, 15 percent—about 4 million people—live in rural areas. Many of these Texans live on farms and in small desert towns, far from major cities and even other small towns. In the past, this distance left them isolated from the rest of the world in many ways. However, the Internet and other modern technology have changed this. With the touch of a button, a person on a Texas ranch can talk with a person in Tokyo, Japan. Current events, cutting-edge technology, and a wealth of valuable skills are just as easy to access. This opens up endless possibilities in business, education, and personal connections for people in even the most isolated of communities.

More than 2.2 million people call Houston (bottom) home. Rural towns in Texas may be 10 miles (16 km) or more from the nearest supermarket.

Texan Tastes

Texas's local cuisine is known as Tex-Mex. It offers an American twist on Mexican dishes such as nachos, tacos, and huevos rancheros. The state also prides itself on local barbecue and chili made from Texas-raised beef. Texas chili can be very spicy, and unlike many other types of chili, it never includes beans. Along the Gulf Coast, many Texans enjoy freshly caught seafood.

  ## Texas Chili

Ask an adult to help you!

Feel free to adjust the spiciness to your own tastes!

Ingredients
2 tablespoons olive oil
5 cloves garlic, minced
2 onions, diced
1 1/2 pounds ground beef
Salt and pepper to taste
2 tablespoons red chili powder (or to taste)

4 plum tomatoes, peeled and diced
1/2 cup tomato paste
2 cups beef stock
3/4 teaspoon ground cumin
2 teaspoons oregano
1/4 cup minced parsley

Directions
With an adult's help, heat the oil in a saucepan over medium-high heat. Add the garlic and onions and cook for about 5 minutes. Add the beef. Stir until it is browned. Drain the fat from the pan, and then add the salt, pepper, and chili powd[er] Cook for 2 minutes. Add the rest of the ingredients. Bring the chili to a simmer, co[ver] the pan, and turn down the heat. Cook for about an hour, stirring occasionally.

Texans welcome U.S. Navy sailors home after a long mission abroad.

Why the State Is Great

Texas's economy made about $1.5 trillion in 2016. That is about as much as was made in Canada, the country with the 10th-largest economy in the world! Texas is filled with creative and inspiring people. It is a place where important business decisions are made. They can impact people around the world. It is also a state filled with natural beauty and farmland. All these things are what make Texas such an amazing state! ★

Famous People

Dwight D. Eisenhower

(1890–1969) was the 34th president of the United States, serving from 1953 to 1961. He was born in Denison.

Lyndon B. Johnson

(1908–1973) was the 36th president of the United States, serving from 1963 to 1969. He was born in Stonewall and continued living there after his time in office.

Alvin Ailey

(1931–1989) was a world-famous dancer and choreographer. His company, the Alvin Ailey American Dance Theater, remains active today. Ailey was born in Rogers.

Willie Nelson

(1933–) is a singer-songwriter and one of the most popular and critically acclaimed country music artists of all time. He was born in Abbott.

Richard Linklater

(1960–) is a film and television producer, director, writer, and actor. He grew up in Huntsville and later lived in Houston and Austin.

Robert Rodriguez

(1968–) is a filmmaker and musician who is best known for writing and directing such films as *Desperado* and the *Spy Kids* series. He is a lifelong Texas resident.

Matthew McConaughey

(1969–) is an Academy Award-winning actor who has appeared in many films and TV series. He was born in Uvalde and lives in Austin.

Erykah Badu

(1971–) is a Grammy Award-winning singer-songwriter. She is a Dallas native.

Eva Longoria

(1975–) is an actress who is best known for her roles on television series such as *Desperate Housewives* and *The Young and the Restless*. She is from Corpus Christi.

Usher

(1978–) is a singer, songwriter, dancer, and actor who has sold millions of albums and earned widespread acclaim. He is from Dallas.

Beyoncé

(1981–) is a singer, songwriter, and actress who is one of the best-selling music artists of all time. She is from Houston.

Miranda Lambert

(1983–) is a singer-songwriter who has had many hits as a solo artist and with her group, the Pistol Annies. She was born in Longview.

Did You Know That ..

Texas covers 268,581 square miles (695,622 square kilometers). That is more than Ohio, Indiana, Maine, New Hampshire, Rhode Island, Vermont, Connecticut, New York, New Jersey, Maryland, Delaware, and Pennsylvania combined!

Texas is home to 14 national park areas, covering 1,244,635 acres (503,686 hectares). This is 0.7 percent of the state's total area.

Texas's highest point is Guadalupe Peak, at a height of 8,749 feet (2,667 meters) above sea level. Its lowest point is sea level along the Gulf of Mexico.

The home in Denton where Dwight D. Eisenhower was born is now a state historic site.

Did you find the truth?

T Texas was once an independent country.

F Texas is the largest state in the country.

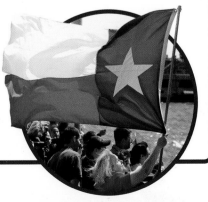

Resources

Books

Nonfiction

Gendell, Megan. *The Spanish Missions of Texas*. New York: Children's Press, 2010.

Walker, Paul Robert. *Remember the Alamo: Texians, Tejanos, and Mexicans Tell Their Stories*. Washington, DC: National Geographic, 2015.

Fiction

Kelly, Jaqueline. *The Evolution of Calpurnia Tate*. New York: Henry Holt, 2009.

Sachar, Louis. *Holes*. New York: Dell Laurel-Leaf Books, 2001.

Movies

Boyhood (2014)

Holes (2003)

Pee-wee's Big Adventure (1985)

Rio Bravo (1959)

Rio Grande (1950)

The Searchers (1956)

Visit this Scholastic website for more information on Texas:

★ www.factsfornow.scholastic.com
Enter the keyword **Texas**

Important Words

annexed (AN-eksd) taken control of by a country or territory

colonies (KAH-luh-neez) communities settled in a new land but with ties to another government

Confederacy (kuhn-FED-ur-uh-see) the group of 11 states that declared independence from the rest of the United States just before the Civil War

counties (KOUN-teez) divisions of a state with their own local governments

drought (DROUT) a long period without rain

mammoths (MAM-uhths) animals that looked like large elephants, with long, curved tusks and shaggy hair

missions (MISH-uhnz) churches or other places where missionaries live and work

nomadic (noh-MAD-ik) traveling from place to place instead of living in the same place all the time

republic (ri-PUHB-lik) a form of government in which the people elect representatives who manage the government

species (SPEE-sheez) one of the groups into which animals and plants of the same genus are divided

Index

Page numbers in **bold** indicate illustrations.

About the Author

Josh Gregory is the author of more than 100 books for kids. He has written about everything from animals to technology to history. A graduate of the University of Missouri–Columbia, he currently lives in Portland, Oregon.

NOV 1 6 2018